D0429281

COMFORT FROM GOD

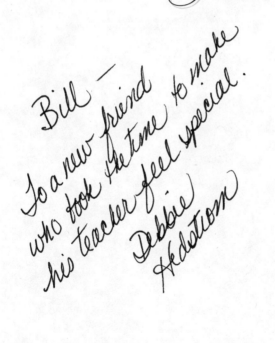

Bill —
To a new friend
who took the time to make
his teacher feel special.
Debbie
Hedstrom

Look at the birds of the air;
they do not sow or reap or store away in barns,
and yet your heavenly Father feeds them.
Are you not much more valuable
than they?

MATTHEW 6:26

JUST THE RIGHT WORDS SERIES

Comfort from God

Scriptural Refreshment
in Times of Need

MULTNOMAH BOOKS · SISTERS, OREGON

JUST THE RIGHT WORDS: COMFORT FROM GOD
published by Multnomah Books
a part of the Questar publishing family

© 1996 by Questar Publishers, Inc.

Edited by Melody Carlson and Deborah Hedstrom
Cover illustration by Sudi McCollum
Design by David Uttley

International Standard Book Number: 1-57673-005-0

Printed in the United States of America

Scripture quotations are from:
The Holy Bible, New International Version (NIV)
© 1973, 1984 by International Bible Society,
used by permission of Zondervan Publishing House

New American Standard Bible (NASB)
© 1960, 1977 by the Lockman Foundation

The New King James Version (NKJV)
© 1984 by Thomas Nelson, Inc.

The King James Version (KJV)

The Living Bible (TLB)
© 1971 by Tyndale House Publishers

For information:
QUESTAR PUBLISHERS, INC. • POST OFFICE BOX 1720 • SISTERS, OREGON 97759

96 97 98 99 00 01 02 03 — 10 9 8 7 6 5 4 3 2 1

CONTENTS

The God of all Comfort
Shall Comfort You...

*T*here come times in our lives when we all long to be comforted. Times when it feels like our world is caving in, or life makes no sense, or we simply want to give up...

As a young child, you may remember the time you were frightened by a nighttime terror, and the only place you felt safe and secure was under the snug protection of your parents' downy quilt. Then as you grew older, your need to be comforted may have become less frequent and not so childish—but perhaps more dire, more urgent.

In the grown-up world we need a stronger source of comfort, and yet we often forget where to look. It's so easy to become distracted by our own trouble and heartache. And we often lose sight of how much our Heavenly Father yearns to draw us into his comfort—how he desires to gather us in his arms and speak the words of life to our frightened hearts. Only God can comfort us with just the right words—words

7

that minister hope and restoration in our darkest moments of need.

Come and allow God's words to enfold you and hold you—to comfort you like nothing else can. Wrap yourself up in them and snuggle down in the same way you once sought refuge under the folds of that big, fluffy quilt.

The God of All Comfort
Shall Comfort You...

WHEN
YOU LONG FOR
A REFUGE

Your Word has been my comfort.
...For these laws of yours
have been my source of joy and singing
through all these years
of my earthly pilgrimage.
...I would have despaired and perished
unless your laws had been my deepest delight....
In my distress and anguish
your commandments comfort me.

PSALM 119:52, 54, 92, 143 (TLB)

Understand, therefore,
that the Lord your God
is the faithful God
who for a thousand generations
keeps his promises
and constantly loves those who love him
and who obey his commands.

DEUTERONOMY 7:9 (TLB)

...The earth and sky begin to shake.
But to his people,
the Lord will be very gentle.
He is their Refuge
and Strength.

JOEL 3:16 (TLB)

...The Lord longs
to be gracious to you,
and therefore
He waits on high
to have compassion on you.

ISAIAH 30:18 (NASB)

The eternal God
is your Refuge,
And underneath
are the everlasting arms.

DEUTERONOMY 33:27 (NKJV)

Praise be to the God
and Father of our Lord Jesus Christ,
the Father of compassion
and the God of all comfort,
who comforts us in all our troubles,
so that we can comfort those in any trouble
with the comfort we ourselves
have received from God.

2 CORINTHIANS 1:3-4 (NIV)

Shout for joy,
O heavens!
And rejoice,
O earth!
Break forth into joyful shouting,
O mountains!
For the LORD has comforted His people,
and will have compassion
on His afflicted.

ISAIAH 49:13 (NASB)

The God of All Comfort
Shall Comfort You...

WHEN YOU ARE
OVERWHELMED

Those who know your name
will trust in you,
for you, Lord,
have never forsaken those who seek you.

PSALM 9:10 (NIV)

I will rejoice and be glad
in Thy lovingkindness,
Because Thou hast seen my affliction;
Thou hast known
the troubles of my soul.

PSALM 31:7 (NASB)

You, who have shown me
great and severe troubles,
Shall revive me again,
And bring me up again
from the depths of the earth.

You shall increase my greatness,
And comfort me
on every side.

PSALM 71:20-21 (NKJV)

"Because he loves me,"
says the LORD,
"I will rescue him;
I will protect him,
for he acknowledges my name.
He will call upon me,
and I will answer him;
I will be with him in trouble,
I will deliver him and honor him."

PSALM 91:14-15 (NIV)

Lord,
when doubts fill my mind,
when my heart is in turmoil,
quiet me
and give me renewed hope
and cheer.

PSALM 94:19 (TLB)

Can a mother forget
the baby at her breast
and have no compassion
on the child she has borne?
Though she may forget,
I will not forget you!
See, I have engraved you
on the palms of my hands;
your walls are ever before me.

ISAIAH 49:15-16 (NIV)

Though I walk in the midst of trouble,
You will revive me;
You will stretch out Your hand
Against the wrath of my enemies,
And Your right hand will save me....

The LORD will perfect
that which concerns me;
Your mercy, O LORD,
endures forever.

PSALM 138:7-8 (NKJV)

"The Lord your God in your midst,
the Mighty One,
will save;
He will rejoice over you
with gladness,
He will quiet you
with His love,
he will rejoice over you
with singing."

ZEPHANIAH 3:17 (NKJV)

"…I have upheld [you]
since you were conceived
and have carried [you]
since your birth.
Even to your old age and gray hairs
I am he,
I am he who will sustain you.
I have made you
and I will carry you;
I will sustain you and
I will rescue you.

ISAIAH 46:3-4 (NIV)

"Thus says the LORD
who made the earth,
the LORD who formed it to establish it—
the LORD is His name,
'Call to Me,
and I will answer you,
and I will tell you great
and mighty things,
which you do not know.' "

JEREMIAH 33:2-3 (NASB)

He will feed his flock
like a shepherd;
he will carry the lambs
in his arms
and gently lead the ewes with young.

Who else
has held the oceans in his hands
and measured off the heavens
with his ruler?

Who else
knows the weight of all the earth
and weighs the mountains
and the hills?

ISAIAH 40:11-12 (TLB)

For I know the thoughts
that I think toward you,
says the LORD,
thoughts of peace
and not of evil,
to give you a future
and a hope.

Then you will call upon Me
and go and pray to Me,
and I will listen to you.

And you will seek Me
and find Me,
when you search for Me
with all your heart.

JEREMIAH 29:11-13 (NKJV)

"You men who are fathers—
if your boy asks for bread,
do you give him a stone?
If he asks for fish,
do you give him a snake?
If he asks for an egg,
do you give him a scorpion?
Of course not!

"And if even sinful persons like yourselves
give children what they need,
don't you realize
that your heavenly Father
will do at least as much,
and give the Holy Spirit
to those who ask for him?"

LUKE 11:11-13 (TLB)

Then He [Jesus] said to them,
"My soul is exceedingly sorrowful,
even to death.
Stay here and watch."

He went a little farther,
and fell on the ground,
and prayed that if it were possible,
the hour might pass from Him.

And He said, "Abba, Father,
all things are possible for You.
Take this cup away from Me;
nevertheless, not what I will,
but what You will."

MARK 14:34-36 (NKJV)

"I have told you all this
so that you will have
peace of heart
and mind.
Here on earth
you will have many trials and sorrows;
but cheer up,
for I have overcome the world."

JOHN 16:33 (TLB)

Though he brings grief,
he will show compassion,
so great is his unfailing love.

For he does not willingly bring
affliction or grief
to the children of men.

LAMENTATIONS 3:32-33 (NIV)

Oh, the depth of the riches
of the wisdom
and knowledge of God!
How unsearchable his judgments,
and his paths beyond tracing out!

"Who has known the mind of the Lord?
Or who has been his counselor?"
"Who has ever given to God,
that God should repay him?"

For from him
and through him
and to him are all things.

ROMANS 11:33-36 (NIV)

"I am the Lord,
the God of all mankind.
Is anything too hard for me?"

JEREMIAH 32:27 (NIV)

Cast all your anxiety on him
because he cares for you.

1 PETER 5:7 (NIV)

Therefore we do not lose heart.
Though outwardly we are wasting away,
yet inwardly
we are being renewed
day by day.

For our light and momentary troubles
are achieving for us
an eternal glory
that far outweighs them all.

So we fix our eyes not on what is seen,
but on what is unseen.
For what is seen is temporary,
but what is unseen
is eternal.

2 CORINTHIANS 4:16-18 (NIV)

Blessed be
the God and Father of our Lord Jesus Christ,
the Father of mercies
and the God of all comfort;
who comforts us in all our afflictions
so that we may be able to comfort
those who are in any affliction
with the comfort
with which we ourselves
are comforted by God.

2 CORINTHIANS 1:3-4 (NASB)

The prospect of the righteous is joy.

PROVERBS 10:28 (NIV)

You have heard of the endurance of Job
and have seen the outcome
of the Lord's dealings,
that the Lord is full of compassion
and is merciful.

And the LORD restored the fortunes of Job
when he prayed for his friends,
and the LORD increased
all that Job had twofold.

JAMES 5:11 AND JOB 42:10 (NASB)

…You have been chosen by God himself—
you are priests of the King,
you are holy and pure,
you are God's very own—
all this so that you may show to others
how God called you
out of the darkness into his wonderful light.

Once you were less than nothing;
now you are God's own.
Once you knew very little
of God's kindness;
now your very lives
have been changed by it.

1 PETER 2:9-10 (TLB)

The God of All Comfort
Shall Comfort You...

WHEN
DEATH COMES
NEAR

My soul weeps because of grief;
Strengthen me
according to Thy word.

PSALM 119:28 (NASB)

All your waves and billows have gone over me,
and floods of sorrow pour upon me
like a thundering cataract.

Yet day by day
the Lord also pours out his steadfast love
upon me,
and through the night
I sing his songs and pray to God
who gives me life.

PSALM 42:7-8 (TLB)

He heals the brokenhearted
and binds up their wounds.

He counts the number of the stars;
he calls them all by name.

Great is our Lord,
and mighty in power;
his understanding is infinite.

PSALM 147:3-5 (NKJV)

He is despised
and rejected by men,
A Man of sorrows
and acquainted with grief....

Surely He has borne our griefs
And carried our sorrows;
Yet we esteemed Him stricken,
Smitten by God, and afflicted.

But He was wounded
for our transgressions,
He was bruised for our iniquities;
The chastisement for our peace
was upon Him,
and by His stripes we are healed.

ISAIAH 53:3-5 (NKJV)

Precious in the sight of the LORD
is the death of his saints.

PSALM 116:15 (KJV)

O my Comforter in sorrow,
my heart is faint within me.

JEREMIAH 8:18 (NIV)

It is vain
for you to rise up early,
to sit up late,
to eat the bread of sorrows:
for so he giveth
his beloved sleep.

PSALM 127:2 (KJV)

The ransomed of the LORD will return.
They will enter Zion with singing;
everlasting joy will crown their heads.
Gladness and joy will overtake them,
and sorrow and sighing will flee away.
"I, even I, am he who comforts you."

ISAIAH 51:11-12 (NIV)

May we be refreshed
as by streams in the desert.
Those who sow tears
shall reap joy.
Yes, they go out weeping,
carrying seed for sowing,
and return singing,
carrying their sheaves.

PSALM 126:4-6 (TLB)

For you will not leave me
among the dead;
you will not allow your beloved one
to rot in the grave.
You have let me experience the joys of life
and the exquisite pleasures
of your own eternal presence.

PSALM 16:10-11 (TLB)

The righteous man perishes...
while no one understands.
For the righteous man is taken away from evil,
He enters into peace,
They rest in their beds,
Each one who walked in his upright way.

ISAIAH 57:1-2 (NASB)

He has sent me
to tell those who mourn
that the time of God's favor to them has come,
and the day of his wrath to their enemies.

To all who mourn in Israel he will give:
Beauty for ashes;
Joy instead of mourning;
Praise instead of heaviness.

For God has planted them
like strong and graceful oaks
for his own glory.

ISAIAH 61:2-3 (TLB)

He will swallow up death
for all time,
And the Lord God
will wipe tears away from all faces.

ISAIAH 25:8 (NASB)

Blessed are they that mourn:
for they shall be comforted.

MATTHEW 5:4 (KJV)

"O death,
where is your victory?
O death,
where is your sting?"

The sting of death is sin,
and the power of sin is the law;
but thanks be to God,
who gives us the victory
through our Lord Jesus Christ.

1 CORINTHIANS 15:55-57 (NASB)

Blessed are the pure in heart:
for they shall see God.

MATTHEW 5:8 (KJV)

"In My Father's house
are many mansions;
if it were not so,
I would have told you.
I go to prepare a place for you.

"And if I go and prepare a place for you,
I will come again
and receive you to Myself;
that where I am, there you may be also."

JOHN 14:2-3 (NKJV)

…We do not want you to be ignorant
about those who fall asleep,
or to grieve like the rest of men, who have no hope.…

According to the Lord's own word,
we tell you that we who are still alive,
who are left till the coming of the Lord,
will certainly not precede those who
have fallen asleep.

For the Lord himself will come
down from heaven, with a loud command,
with the voice of the archangel
and with the trumpet call of God,
and the dead in Christ will rise first.

Therefore encourage each other with these words.

1 THESSALONIANS 4:13, 15, 16, 18 (NIV)

And I heard a loud voice from the throne saying,
"Now the dwelling of God is with men,
and he will live with them.
They will be his people, and God himself
will be with them and be their God.
He will wipe every tear from their eyes.
There will be no more death
or mourning or crying or pain,
for the old order of things has passed away."

REVELATION 21:3-4 (NIV)

So we are always confident,
knowing that
while we are at home in the body
we are absent from the Lord...
To be absent from the body...
[is] to be present with the Lord.

2 CORINTHIANS 5:6, 8 (NKJV)

The God of All Comfort
Shall Comfort You...

WHEN
LIFE PRESSES
IN

He led you through the vast
and dreadful desert,
that thirsty and waterless land,
with its venomous snakes
and scorpions.
He brought you water out of hard rock.
He gave you manna to eat in the desert,
something your fathers had never known,
to humble and to test you
so that in the end
it might go well with you.

DEUTERONOMY 8:15-16 (NIV)

Just as a father
has compassion on his children,
so the Lord
has compassion on those who fear Him.

For He Himself
knows our frame;
He is mindful that we are but dust.

As for man,
his days are like grass;
As a flower of the field, so he flourishes.
When the wind has passed over it,
it is no more;
And its place acknowledges it no longer.

But the lovingkindness of the LORD
is from everlasting to everlasting
on those who fear Him.

PSALM 103:13-17 (NASB)

"For You are my lamp,
O Lord;
The Lord shall enlighten my darkness.

For by You
I can run against a troop;
By my God I can leap over a wall."

2 SAMUEL 22:29-30 (NKJV)

If God be for us,
who can be against us?

ROMANS 8:31 (KJV)

The Lord is gracious
and compassionate,
slow to anger
and rich in love.

The LORD is good to all;
he has compassion on all he has made.

PSALM 145:8-9 (NIV)

He will be very gracious to you at
the sound of your cry;
When He hears it,
He will answer you.

And though the Lord gives you
The bread of adversity and the water of affliction,
Yet your teachers will not be moved....
Your ears shall hear a word behind you, saying,
"This is the way, walk in it."

ISAIAH 30:19-21 (NKJV)

No temptation has overtaken you
but such as is common to man;
and God is faithful,
who will not allow you to be tempted
beyond what you are able,
but with the temptation
will provide the way of escape also,
that you may be able to endure it.

1 CORINTHIANS 10:13 (NASB)

But Simon answered and said to Him,
"Master, we have toiled all night and caught nothing;
nevertheless at Your word
I will let down the net."
And when they had done this,
they caught a great number of fish,
and their net was breaking.

LUKE 5:5-6 (NKJV)

"Ah, Lord GOD! Behold,
You have made the heavens and the earth
by Your great power and outstretched arm.
There is nothing too hard for You."

JEREMIAH 32:17 (NKJV)

Blessed is the man who perseveres under trial,
because when he has stood the test,
he will receive the crown of life
that God has promised to those who love him.

JAMES 1:12 (NIV)

And since we are his children,
we will share his treasures—
for all God gives to his Son Jesus is now ours too.
But if we are to share his glory,
we must also share his suffering.
Yet what we suffer now
is nothing compared to the glory he will give us later.

ROMANS 8:17-18 (TLB)

…We are more than conquerors through
him that loved us.

For I am persuaded, that neither death,
nor life,
nor angels,
nor principalities,
nor powers,
nor things present,
nor things to come,
nor height,
nor depth,
nor any other creature,
shall be able to separate us from the love of God,
which is in Christ Jesus our LORD.

ROMANS 8:37-39 (KJV)

For we do not have a high priest
who cannot sympathize with our weaknesses,
but one who has been tempted in all things
as we are, yet without sin.

Let us therefore draw near
with confidence to the throne of grace,
that we may receive mercy
and may find grace to help in time of need.

HEBREWS 4:15-16 (NASB)

God also bound himself
with an oath,
so that those he promised to help
would be perfectly sure
and never need to wonder
whether he might change his plans.
He has given us both his promise
and his oath,
two things we can completely count on,
for it is impossible
for God to tell a lie.

HEBREWS 6:17-18 (TLB)

I wait for the LORD,
my soul does wait,
And in His word
do I hope.

PSALM 130:5 (NASB)

We have this hope
as an anchor for the soul,
firm and secure.

HEBREWS 6:19 (NIV)

" 'I am coming quickly;
hold fast what you have,
in order that no one take your crown.
'He who overcomes,
I will make him a pillar in the temple of My God,
and he will not go out from it anymore;
and I will write upon him the name of My God.' "

REVELATION 3:11-12 (NASB)

Now may our Lord Jesus Christ Himself
and God our Father, who has loved us
and given us eternal comfort and good hope by grace,
comfort and strengthen your hearts
in every good work and word.

2 THESSALONIANS 2:16-17 (NASB)

The God of All Comfort
Shall Comfort You...

WHEN YOU ARE
AFRAID

"Fear not, for I have redeemed you;
I have called you by your name;
You are Mine.
When you pass through the waters,
I will be with you;
And through the rivers, they shall not overflow you.
When you walk through the fire,
you shall not be burned,
Nor shall the flame scorch you.
For I am the LORD your God,
The Holy One of Israel, your Savior."

ISAIAH 43:1-3 (NKJV)

We live within the shadow
of the Almighty,
sheltered by the God
who is above all gods.

This I declare,
that he alone is my refuge,
my place of safety;
he is my God,
and I am trusting him.

For he rescues you from every trap,
and protects you from the fatal plague.
He will shield you with his wings!
They will shelter you.
His faithful promises are your armor.

Now you don't need to be afraid
of the dark any more,
nor fear the dangers of the day;
nor dread the plagues of darkness,
nor disasters in the morning.

PSALM 91:1-6 (TLB)

Do not be afraid
of sudden terror,
Nor of trouble from the wicked
when it comes;
For the LORD
will be your confidence,
And will keep your foot
from being caught.

PROVERBS 3:25-26 (NKJV)

I am the First and Last;
there is no other God.

Who else can tell you
what is going to happen
in the days ahead?
Let them tell you
if they can, and prove their power.
Let them do as I have done
since ancient times.

Don't, don't be afraid.
Haven't I proclaimed from ages past
[that I would save you?]
You are my witnesses—is there any other God?
No!
None that I know about!
There is no other Rock!

ISAIAH 44:6-8 (TLB)

There is no fear in love;
but perfect love casts out fear,
because fear involves punishment,
and the one who fears
is not perfected in love.
We love,
because He first loved us.

1 JOHN 4:18-19 (NASB)

God is our refuge and strength,
A very present help in trouble.

Therefore we will not fear,
though the earth should change,
And though the mountains slip
into the heart of the sea.

PSALM 46:1-2 (NASB)

"The Lord is my helper;
I will not be afraid.
What can man do to me?"

HEBREWS 13:6 (NIV)

"Are not five sparrows sold for two cents?
And yet not one of them
is forgotten before God.
"Indeed, the very hairs of your head are all numbered.
Do not fear;
you are of more value than many sparrows."

LUKE 12:6-7 (NASB)

"Do not be afraid;
for God has come in order to test you,
and in order that the fear of Him
may remain with you,
so that you may not sin."

EXODUS 20:20 (NASB)

"I am leaving you with a gift—
peace of mind and heart!
And the peace I give isn't fragile
like the peace the world gives.
So don't be troubled or afraid."

JOHN 14:27 (TLB)

"Do not be afraid, O Zion;
Do not let your hands fall limp.

"The LORD your God is in your midst,
A victorious warrior.
He will exult over you with joy,
He will be quiet in His love,
He will rejoice over you
with shouts of joy."

ZEPHANIAH 3:16-17 (NASB)

Even though I walk
through the valley of the shadow of death,
I fear no evil;
for Thou art with me.

PSALM 23:4 (NASB)

" 'Do not fear, for I am with you;
Do not anxiously look about you,
for I am your God.
I will strengthen you, surely I will help you,
Surely I will uphold you
with My righteous right hand....'

"For I am the LORD your God,
who upholds your right hand,
Who says to you,
'Do not fear, I will help you.' "

ISAIAH 41:10, 13 (NASB)

The God of All Comfort
Shall Comfort You...

WHEN
YOU WANT TO
GIVE UP

For the eyes of the Lord
search back and forth across the whole earth,
looking for people
whose hearts are perfect toward him,
so that he can show his great power
in helping them.

2 CHRONICLES 16:9 (TLB)

I am in deep trouble and I need his help so badly.
All night long I pray,
lifting my hands to heaven, pleading.
There can be no joy for me until he acts.

I think of God and moan,
overwhelmed with longing for his help.
I cannot sleep until you act.
I am too distressed even to pray!...

Has the Lord rejected me forever?
Will he never again be favorable?
Is his lovingkindness gone forever?
Has his promise failed?...

I recall the many miracles he did for me so long ago.
Those wonderful deeds are constantly in my thoughts.
I cannot stop thinking about them.
O God, your ways are holy.
Where is there any other as mighty as you?

PSALM 77:2-4, 7-8, 11-13 (TLB)

And in the same way—by our faith—
the Holy Spirit helps us
with our daily problems
and in our praying.
For we don't even know what we should pray for
nor how to pray as we should;
but the Holy Spirit prays for us
with such feeling
that it cannot be expressed in words.

And the Father who knows all hearts knows,
of course, what the Spirit is saying
as he pleads for us in harmony with God's own will.

And we know that all that happens to us is working
for our good if we love God
and are fitting into his plans.

ROMANS 8:26-28 (TLB)

On my bed I remember you;
I think of you
through the watches of the night.

Because you are my help,
I sing in the shadow of your wings.

My soul clings to you;
your right hand upholds me.

PSALM 63:6-8 (NIV)

The good man
does not escape all troubles—
he has them too.

But the Lord helps him
in each and every one.

PSALM 34:19 (TLB)

The steps of a good man
are ordered by the Lord,
And He delights in his way.

Though he fall,
he shall not be utterly cast down;
for the LORD upholds him
with His hand.

PSALM 37:23-24 (NKJV)

My help comes from the Lord,
Who made heaven and earth.

He will not allow your foot to be moved;
He who keeps you
will not slumber.
Behold, He who keeps Israel
Shall neither slumber nor sleep.

The LORD is your keeper;
The LORD is your shade at your right hand.
The sun shall not strike you by day,
Nor the moon by night.
The LORD shall preserve you from all evil;
He shall preserve your soul.
The LORD shall preserve your going out
and your coming in
From this time forth,
and even forevermore.

PSALM 121:2-8 (NKJV)

You have seen me tossing and turning
through the night.
You have collected all my tears
and preserved them in your bottle!
You have recorded every one
in your book.

The very day I call for help,
the tide of battle turns.
My enemies flee!
This one thing I know: God is for me!

PSALM 56:8-9 (TLB)

I weep with grief;
my heart is heavy with sorrow;
encourage and cheer me
with your words.

Keep me far from every wrong;
help me, undeserving as I am,
to obey your laws....

Lord, don't let me make a mess of things.
If you will only help me
to want your will,
then I will follow your laws even more closely.
Just tell me what to do and I will do it, Lord.
As long as I live
I'll wholeheartedly obey.
Make me walk along the right paths,
for I know how delightful they really are....

Revive my heart toward you.

PSALM 119:28-29, 31-35, 37 (TLB)

…Now for a little while
you may have had to suffer grief in all kinds of trials.
These have come so that your faith—
of greater worth than gold,
which perishes even though refined by fire—
may be proved genuine
and may result in praise, glory and honor
when Jesus Christ is revealed.

1 PETER 1:6-7 (NIV)

Whom have I in heaven but thee?
and there is none upon earth
that I desire beside thee.

My flesh and my heart faileth:
but God is the strength of my heart,
and my portion forever.

PSALM 73:25-26 (KJV)

From the end of the earth I call to Thee,
when my heart is faint;
Lead me to the rock that is higher than I.
For Thou hast been a refuge for me,
a tower of strength....

PSALM 61:2-3 (NASB)

Give your burdens to the Lord.
He will carry them.
He will not permit the godly to slip or fall.

PSALM 55:22 (TLB)

In the day when I cried out,
You answered me,
And made me bold
with strength in my soul.

PSALM 138:3 (NKJV)

The Lord sustains all who fall,
And raises up all
who are bowed down.
The eyes of all look to Thee....

The Lord is righteous in all His ways,
And kind in all His deeds.
The Lord is near to all who call upon Him,
To all who call upon Him in truth.

He will fulfill the desire
of those who fear Him;
He will also hear their cry
and will save them.
The LORD keeps all who love Him.

PSALM 145:14-15, 17-20 (NASB)

The God of All Comfort
Shall Comfort You...

WHEN YOU
GROW WEARY

"For six days work may be done,
but on the seventh day you shall have a holy day,
a sabbath of complete rest to the Lord."

EXODUS 35:2 (NASB)

He who dwells
in the shelter of the Most High
will rest in the shadow of the Almighty.
I will say of the Lord,
"He is my refuge and my fortress,
my God, in whom I trust."

He will cover you with his feathers,
and under his wings you will find refuge;
his faithfulness will be your shield
and rampart.

PSALM 91:1-2, 4 (NIV)

O God, you are my God,
earnestly I seek you;
my soul thirsts for you, my body longs for you,
in a dry and weary land where there is no water.

I have seen you in the sanctuary
and beheld your power and your glory.

Because your love is better than life,
my lips will glorify you.

PSALM 63:1-3 (NIV)

You gave abundant showers, O God;
you refreshed your weary inheritance.

PSALM 68:9 (NIV)

Be at rest once more,
O my soul,
for the Lord has been good to you.

For you, O LORD,
have delivered my soul from death,
my eyes from tears,
my feet from stumbling,
that I may walk before the LORD
in the land of the living.

PSALM 116:7-9 (NIV)

When my spirit grows faint within me,
it is you who know my way.

PSALM 142:3 (NIV)

So my spirit grows faint within me;
my heart within me is dismayed.

I remember the days of long ago;
I meditate on all your works
and consider what your hands have done.
I spread out my hands to you;
my soul thirsts for you like a parched land.

PSALM 143:4-6 (NIV)

"Let the beloved of the Lord
rest secure in him,
for he shields him all day long,
and the one the Lord loves rests
between his shoulders."

DEUTERONOMY 33:12 (NIV)

"For I satisfy the weary ones
and refresh everyone who languishes."

JEREMIAH 31:25 (NASB)

But happy is the man…
whose hope is in the Lord his God—
the God who made both earth and heaven,
the seas and everything in them.

He is the God
who keeps every promise….
He lifts the burdens
from those bent down beneath their loads.
For the Lord loves good men.

PSALM 146:5-6, 8 (TLB)

Hast thou not known?
hast thou not heard,
that the everlasting God,
the Lord,
the Creator of the ends of the earth,
fainteth not,
neither is weary?
There is no searching of his understanding.

He giveth power to the faint;
and to them that have no might
he increaseth strength.
Even the youths shall faint and be weary,
and the young men shall utterly fall:

But they that wait upon the LORD
shall renew their strength;
they shall mount up with wings as eagles;
they shall run, and not be weary;
and they shall walk, and not faint.

ISAIAH 40:28-31 (KJV)

And let us not grow weary
while doing good,
for in due season we shall reap
if we do not lose heart.

GALATIANS 6:9 (NKJV)

Come unto me,
all ye that labour and are heavy laden,
and I will give you rest.

Take my yoke upon you,
and learn of me;
for I am meek and lowly in heart:
and ye shall find rest
unto your souls.

MATTHEW 11:28-29 (KJV)

For I am confident of this very thing,
that He who began a good work in you
will perfect it
until the day of Christ Jesus.

PHILIPPIANS 1:6 (NASB)

So there is a full complete rest
still waiting for the people of God.

Christ has already entered there.
He is resting from his work,
just as God did after the creation.

HEBREWS 4:9-10 (TLB)

Keep your eyes on Jesus,
our leader and instructor.

He was willing to die a shameful death on the cross
because of the joy he knew would be his afterwards;
and now he sits in the place of honor
by the throne of God.

If you want to keep from becoming fainthearted
and weary,
think about his patience
as sinful men did such terrible things to him.
After all, you have never yet struggled against
sin and temptation
until you sweat great drops of blood.

HEBREWS 12:2-4 (TLB)

"My grace is sufficient for you,
for My strength is made perfect in weakness."

2 CORINTHIANS 12:9 (NKJV)

"My Presence will go with you,
and I will give you rest."

EXODUS 33:14 (NKJV)

"Stand in the ways and see,
And ask for the old paths,
where the good way is,
And walk in it;
Then you will find rest for your souls."

JEREMIAH 6:16 (NKJV)

The God of All Comfort
Shall Comfort You...

WHEN THE
WAITING BECOMES
LONG

I would have lost heart,
unless I had believed
That I would see
the goodness of the Lord
In the land of the living.

Wait on the LORD;
Be of good courage,
And He shall strengthen your heart;
Wait, I say,
on the LORD!

PSALM 27:13-14 (NKJV)

But the eyes of the Lord
are on those who fear him,
on those whose hope is
in his unfailing love....

We wait in hope
for the Lord;
he is our help and our shield.
In him our hearts rejoice,
for we trust in his holy name.

May your unfailing love
rest upon us,
O LORD,
even as we put our hope
in you.

PSALM 33:18, 20-22 (NIV)

Rest in the Lord
and wait patiently for Him;
Do not fret because of him
who prospers in his way,
Because of the man
who carries out wicked schemes.
Cease from anger,
and forsake wrath;
Do not fret,
it leads only to evildoing.

PSALM 37:7-8 (NASB)

Love is very patient and kind.

1 CORINTHIANS 13:4 (TLB)

I waited patiently for God
to help me;
then he listened
and heard my cry.

He lifted me
out of the pit of despair,
out from the bog
and the mire,
and set my feet
on a hard, firm path
and steadied me
as I walked along.
He has given me
a new song to sing,
of praises to our God.

Many blessings are given
to those who trust the Lord.

PSALM 40:1-4 (TLB)

My soul waits for the Lord
More than those who watch for the morning—
Yes, more than those who watch for the morning.

O Israel, hope in the LORD;
For with the LORD there is mercy,
And with Him is abundant redemption.

PSALM 130:6-7 (NKJV)

In the morning,
O Lord,
you hear my voice;
in the morning
I lay my requests
before you
and wait
in expectation.

PSALM 5:3 (NIV)

My soul,
wait silently for God alone,
For my expectation is from Him.

He only is my rock
and my salvation;
He is my defense;
I shall not be moved.

In God
is my salvation
and my glory;
The rock of my strength,
And my refuge,
is in God.

Trust in Him
at all times, you people;
Pour out your heart before Him;
God is a refuge for us.

PSALM 62:5-8 (NKJV)

I wait for the LORD,
my soul does wait,
And in His word
do I hope.

PSALM 130:5 (NASB)

You will keep him in perfect peace,
Whose mind is stayed on You,
Because he trusts in You.

Trust in the LORD forever,
For in YAH, the LORD,
is everlasting strength.

ISAIAH 26:3-4 (NKJV)

The path of the righteous is level;
O upright One,
you make the way of the righteous smooth.
Yes, LORD,
walking in the way of your laws,
we wait for you;
your name and renown
are the desire of our hearts.

ISAIAH 26:7-8 (NIV)

…This I call to mind
and therefore I have hope:
Because of the LORD's great love
we are not consumed,
for his compassions never fail.
They are new
every morning;
great is your faithfulness.

I say to myself,
"The LORD is my portion;
therefore I will wait
for him."
The LORD is good
to those whose hope
is in him,
to the one who seeks him;
it is good to wait quietly
for the salvation of the LORD.

LAMENTATIONS 3:21-26 (NIV)

Therefore the LORD will wait,
that He may be gracious to you;
And therefore
He will be exalted,
that He may have mercy on you.
For the LORD is a God of justice;
Blessed are all those
who wait for Him.

ISAIAH 30:18 (NKJV)

Slowly, steadily, surely,
the time approaches
when the vision will be fulfilled.
If it seems slow, do not despair,
for these things will surely come to pass.
Just be patient!
They will not be overdue a single day!

HABAKKUK 2:3 (TLB)

Now you have every grace and blessing;
every spiritual gift and power
for doing his will
are yours
during this time of waiting
for the return of our Lord Jesus Christ.

And he guarantees right up to the end
that you will be counted free
from all sin and guilt
on that day when he returns.

God will surely do this for you,
for he always does just what he says....

1 CORINTHIANS 1:7-9 (TLB)

But as for me,
I watch in hope for the Lord,
I wait for God my Savior;
my God will hear me.

MICAH 7:7 (NIV)

But you, dear friends,
build yourselves up in your most holy faith
and pray in the Holy Spirit.
Keep yourselves in God's love
as you wait for the mercy
of our Lord Jesus Christ
to bring you to eternal life.

JUDE 20-21 (NIV)

Therefore be patient, brethren,
until the coming of the Lord.

See how the farmer
waits for the precious fruit of the earth,
waiting patiently for it
until it receives the early
and latter rain.

You also be patient.
Establish your hearts,
for the coming of the Lord is at hand.

JAMES 5:7-8 (NKJV)

...For why does one still hope
for what he sees?
But if we hope for what we do not see,
we eagerly wait for it
with perseverance.

ROMANS 8:24-25 (NKJV)

...We wait for the blessed hope—
the glorious appearing of our
great God and Savior, Jesus Christ.

TITUS 2:13 (NIV)

For since the world began
no one has seen or heard of
such a God as ours,
who works for those who wait for him!

ISAIAH 64:4 (TLB)

The God of All Comfort
Shall Comfort You...

WHEN
YOU SEEK THE
ROAD HOME

"...You will seek the Lord
your God,
and you will find Him
if you seek Him
with all your heart
and with all your soul....
"(For the Lord
your God
is a merciful God),
He will not forsake you
nor destroy you,
nor forget the covenant of your fathers.

DEUTERONOMY 4:29, 31 (NKJV)

...Manasseh [King of Judah] seduced them to do evil
more than the nations whom the LORD destroyed
before the sons of Israel.

[Twenty years later,]
...When he was in distress,
he entreated the LORD his God
and humbled himself greatly
before the God of his fathers.
When he prayed to Him,
He was moved by his entreaty
and heard his supplication,
and brought him again to Jerusalem
to his kingdom.

Then Manasseh knew that the LORD was God.

2 KINGS 21:9 AND 2 CHRONICLES 33:12-13 (NASB)

Sing praise to the LORD,
you His godly ones,
And give thanks to His holy name.

For His anger is but for a moment,
His favor is for a lifetime;
Weeping may last for the night,
but a shout of joy
comes in the morning.

PSALM 30:4-5 (NASB)

The LORD has appeared of old to me, saying:
"Yes, I have loved you
with an everlasting love;
Therefore with lovingkindness
I have drawn you."

JEREMIAH 31:3 (NKJV)

Bless the LORD, O my soul,
And forget not all His benefits:
Who forgives all your iniquities,
Who heals all your diseases,
Who redeems your life from destruction,
Who crowns you with lovingkindness
and tender mercies.

PSALM 103:2-4 (NKJV)

The LORD is merciful and gracious....
He has not dealt with us according to our sins,
Nor punished us according to our iniquities.

For as the heavens are high above the earth,
So great is His mercy toward those who fear Him;

As far as the east is from the west,
So far has He removed our transgressions from us.

As a father pities his children,
So the LORD pities those who fear Him.
For He knows our frame;
He remembers that we are dust.

PSALM 103:8, 10-14 (NKJV)

Many times he delivered them,
but they were bent on rebellion
and they wasted away
in their sin.

But he took note of their distress
when he heard their cry;
for their sake
he remembered his covenant
and out of his great love
he relented.

PSALM 106:43-45 (NIV)

But it was only with their words
they followed him,
not with their hearts;
their hearts were far away.
They did not keep their promises.

Yet he was merciful
and forgave their sins
and didn't destroy them all.
Many and many a time
he held back his anger.
For he remembered
that they were merely mortal men,
gone in a moment
like a breath of wind.

PSALM 78:36-39 (TLB)

I know, O Lord,
that your decisions are right
and that your punishment was right
and did me good.

Now let your lovingkindness comfort me,
just as you promised.
Surround me with your tender mercies,
that I may live.
For your law is my delight.

PSALM 119:75-77 (TLB)

He who covers his sins will not prosper,
But whoever confesses and forsakes them
will have mercy.

PROVERBS 28:13 (NKJV)

I will punish their sin with the rod,
their iniquity with flogging;

but I will not take my love from him,
nor will I ever betray
my faithfulness.

PSALM 89:32-33 (NIV)

Rebuke a wise man,
and he will love you.
Give instruction to a wise man,
and he will be still wiser;
Teach a just man,
and he will increase in learning.

PROVERBS 9:8-9 (NKJV)

Who is a God like you,
who pardons sin and forgives
the transgression of the remnant of his inheritance?
You do not stay angry forever
but delight to show mercy.
You will again have compassion on us;
you will tread our sins underfoot
and hurl all our iniquities into the depths of the sea.

MICAH 7:18-19 (NIV)

"But the Lord our God is merciful
and pardons even those
who have rebelled against him."

DANIEL 9:9 (TLB)

I will not execute My fierce anger;
I will not destroy Ephraim again.

For I am God and not man,
the Holy One in your midst,
and I will not come in wrath.

HOSEA 11:9 (NASB)

Therefore I will look to the Lord;
I will wait for the God of my salvation;
My God will hear me.

Do not rejoice over me, my enemy;
When I fall, I will arise;
When I sit in darkness,
the Lord will be a light to me.

I will bear the indignation of the Lord,
Because I have sinned against Him,
Until He pleads my case and executes justice for me.

He will bring me forth to the light;
I will see His righteousness.

MICAH 7:7-9 (NKJV)

O LORD, do not rebuke me in your anger
or discipline me in your wrath.
Be merciful to me, LORD, for I am faint.

PSALM 6:1-2 (NIV)

...You will restore me and make me live.

Indeed it was for my own peace
That I had great bitterness;
But You have lovingly delivered my soul
from the pit of corruption,
For You have cast all my sins behind Your back.

ISAIAH 38:16-17 (NKJV)

[Jesus] said to Simon, "Do you see this woman?
I entered your house;
you gave Me no water for My feet,
but she has wet My feet with her tears,
and wiped them with her hair.

"You gave Me no kiss;
but she, since the time I came in, has not ceased to kiss
My feet.
You did not anoint My head with oil,
but she anointed My feet with perfume.

"For this reason I say to you,
her sins, which are many, have been forgiven,
for she loved much;
but he who is forgiven little, loves little."

LUKE 7:44-47 (NASB)

For God sent not his Son
into the world to condemn the world;
but that the world through him might be saved.

He that believeth on him
is not condemned:
but he that believeth not is condemned already,
because he hath not believed
in the name of the only begotten Son of God.

JOHN 3:17-18 (KJV)

"…While he was still a long way off,
his father saw him
and was filled with compassion for him;
he ran to his son,
threw his arms around him
and kissed him.

"The son said to him,
'Father, I have sinned
against heaven and against you.
I am no longer worthy to be called your son.'

"But the father said to his servants,
'Quick! Bring the best robe and put it on him.
Put a ring on his finger
and sandals on his feet.
Bring the fattened calf and kill it.
Let's have a feast
and celebrate.
For this son of mine was dead
and is alive again;
he was lost and is found.' "

LUKE 15:20-24 (NIV)

So rend your heart,
and not your garments;
Return to the LORD your God,
For He is gracious and merciful,
Slow to anger,
and of great kindness;
And He relents from doing harm.

JOEL 2:13 (NKJV)

But God demonstrates his own love for us in this:
While we were still sinners,
Christ died for us.

ROMANS 5:8 (NIV)

"For a mere moment I have forsaken you,
But with great mercies
I will gather you.
With a little wrath I hid My face from you for a
moment;
But with everlasting kindness
I will have mercy on you,"
Says the LORD,
your Redeemer.

ISAIAH 54:7-8 (NKJV)

God deals with you as with sons;
for what son is there whom his father does
not discipline?
But if you are without discipline,
of which all have become partakers,
then you are illegitimate children
and not sons.

...He disciplines us for our good,
that we may share His holiness.
All discipline for the moment seems not to be joyful,
but sorrowful;
yet to those who have been trained by it,
afterwards it yields the peaceful fruit of righteousness.

HEBREWS 12:7-8, 10-11 (NASB)